50

WAYS TO SAY
YOU'RE
Awesome

Alexandra Franzen

sourcebooks

Published by Sourcebooks, Inc.
P.O. Box 4410, Naperville, Illinois 60567-4410
(630) 961-3900
Fax: (630) 961-2168
www.sourcebooks.com

Printed and bound in China.
LEO 10 9 8 7 6 5 4 3 2 1

To my hero, Mr. Rogers.
I still want to be your neighbor.

This book contains
50 Ways to Say You're AWESOME.
(Who would've guessed?)

Each page is perforated—so you can tear it out, add a lively note to the back, and give it to someone you adore (a friend, a partner—or even yourself).

Need a lil' nudge to get started?
Try this:

50 Ways to Use This Book

1. Choose a note at random. Call a friend. Read the note into their voicemail.
2. Leave a note for your favorite waitress, tucked inside the bill.
3. Place a note in every mailbox on the street.
4. Give a note to the next stranger who smiles at you.
5. Roll the notes into miniature cones and fill them with candy (you'll be very popular).
6. Use each note as a dinner party place card.
7. Leave anonymous mystery-notes inside your coworkers' cubicles.
8. Paste a note inside your scrapbook, wedding album, or photo journal.
9. Tape a note to your bathroom mirror ('cause YOU'RE awesome, too!)
10. Send a note to everyone on your family tree, starting with your immediate clan and radiating outward. (You might need to buy another book. Just sayin'.)
11. Staple a note to the front page of the newspaper and leave it at your local coffee shop. Today's forecast: Awesomeness.
12. Give a note to your best girlfriend every day for 50 days. (She'll flip.)
13. Slip a note to that cutie you've been ogling for ages.
14. Hide notes all around your home for your partner (or roommate) to discover. (It's like Awesome Easter, all year long!)
15. Hand a note to the milk-splattered guy or gal who fixes your morning latte.

16. Save a note in your freezer, for later (just 'cause it's funny).
17. Tuck a note into your sweetheart's coat pocket.
18. Fold a note into a piece of ultra-inspiring origami.
19. Press a note inside a library book, for a future reader to discover.
20. Snap a picture of your favorite note and post it on Facebook, Twitter, or Pinterest.
21. Ask your local baker to decorate a cake, inspired by your favorite note.
22. Pin a note to the bulletin board in your local coffee shop or community hall.
23. Send a note to a celebrity you've admired from afar.
24. Choose your favorite note. Hire a pilot to write the message in the clouds.
25. Flip to a random note. Text the message to everyone you've got on speed dial.
26. Use all 50 notes to papier-mâché The World's Most Encouraging Piñata.
27. Send a note to the last person who did you a favor—small, medium, or major.
28. Tuck a note on every car windshield on your block. (Waaay more fun than parking tickets.)
29. Send a bundle of notes to everyone at your local fire station—with muffins.
30. Put a stack of notes in a public restroom—with a jar of mints.
31. Send a note to your mom—with a bouquet of fresh flowers.
32. Throwing a birthday party? Stick a note in everyone's party favor bag.
33. Fold a note into a paper airplane and send it soaring towards someone who needs a dose of love.
34. Pop a note into your own lunchbox or brown bag. Self-encouragement rules!
35. Roll a note into a scroll and tuck it through a mini-donut. Ultimate fortune cookie!
36. Fold a note into a mini envelope… for another note to rest inside! (Double-awesome!)

37. Keep a secret stash of notes in your glove box, for "emergencies."
38. Hide a note inside a box of winter clothes. Forget about it... then discover it next season.
39. Frame your favorite note and place it on your workspace.
40. Laminate each note and use 'em as drink coasters.
41. Give half the notes to your sweetheart. Keep half for yourself. Exchange notes every day for 25 days.
42. Mail a note to your favorite elementary school teacher.
43. Put a note under your kidlet's pillow... from the Awesome Fairy.
44. Slip a note under your neighbor's door. (Mr. Rogers would approve.)
45. Scatter all 50 notes on your bed, like rose petals. (Just don't float them in the bathtub...)
46. Photograph yourself holding each note. Send all 50 pics to your sweetheart, one at a time.
47. Hide a note (in a snug, watertight box) for a Geocache hunt.
48. Leave a note for your housekeeper, hairstylist, or babysitter—with a fat tip.
49. Mail a note to yourself—in the future.
50. Give the whole dang book to a wildly special friend (tell 'em one single note just wouldn't cut it).

BOOM!
BRILLIANCE STRIKES AGAIN.

To: _____

You're AWESOME because_____

_____

_____

Ooh! And one more thing_____

_____

_____

From: _____

WHEN
YOU'RE
INSANELY FAMOUS,
DON'T FORGET
HOW MUCH
I ADORED YOU

First.

To: _____

In case you forgot: I think you're unbelievably AWESOME.

I appreciate the way you _____

_____.

And how you always _____

_____.

Thank you for adding so much _____

_____ to my life.

Love: _____

FANTASTIC + FABULOUS =

fabulastic.

YEP. THAT'S YOU.

To: _____

You make my life AWESOME in more ways than I can count (and—not to brag—but I can count pretty high). But for starters, here's 5 of 'em:

1. _____

2. _____

3. _____

4. _____

5. _____

I bow to your AWESOMENESS—now and forever.

From: _____

WHERE
DID YOU
PICK UP THOSE
SEXY
MIND-MOVES?

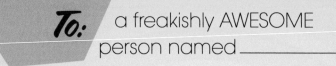

To: a freakishly AWESOME
person named _____

Thank you for always _____

_____

_____

and for proving, once and for all, that _____

_____

_____

You're smashing. And that's final.

Love: _____

You remind me what

Possible

feels like.

To: _____

I bet if you look up "AWESOME" in the dictionary, there's a diagram of your DNA. Made by scientists. Who know things.

As long as I live, I'll never forget the AWESOME way you

_____

_____&_____

_____

THANK YOU barely covers it.

XO. _____

To: _____

FACT:

The world is better with your AWESOMENESS in it.

Thank you for reminding me that _____

_____

and for sharing your _____

_____.

Stay shiny and shimmery-bright.

From: _____

I hereby decree _____

to be Completely and Utterly AWESOME

in Every Conceivable Way.

This proclamation goes into worldwide effect on

_____ at _____ am / pm.

Those who disagree with my proclamation can,

legally speaking, get lost.

Yours
Sincerely,

_____

CEO and President of _____

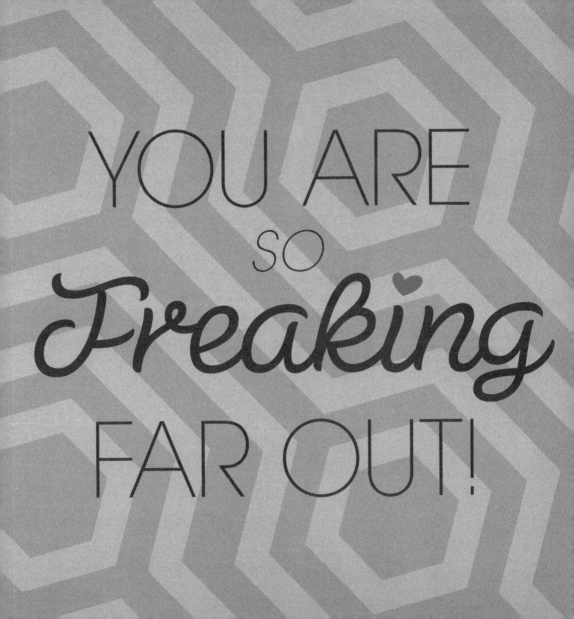

To: _____

Life isn't always easy—but you're always AWESOME.

I admire the way you _____,

even when things are tough.

And if I were President of the World, you'd win a prize for

_____.

Keep on trucking, _____.

You've got a major fan, right here.

Love: _____

YOU'RE THE CAT'S MEOW, THE DOG'S HOWL, AND THE CURMUDGEON'S *harrumph—* ALL ROLLED INTO ONE.

Dear: _____

If I could, I'd rent an airplane

and write **You're AWESOME!** in the clouds.

But, shucks! I forgot to renew my pilot's license.

Instead… here's a quick note:

_____

_____

_____

Your brilliance knows no bounds.

Love: _____

Dear: _____

I'm not sure how you got so AWESOME—

but I'm really glad you did.

I think it's fan-freakin'-tastic that you _____

_____

and I'm so proud of the way you _____

_____.

You are the most _____ person I know.

Put simply? You rule.

XO. _____

You are simply . . .
BEYOND.

To: _____

You're AWESOME because _____

_____

_____

Ooh! And one more thing _____

_____

_____

From: _____

To: _____

In case you forgot: I think you're unbelievably AWESOME.

I appreciate the way you _____

_____.

And how you always _____

_____.

Thank you for adding so much _____

_____ to my life.

Love: _____

DO THEY SELL YOU IN BULK? AND CAN I PREORDER?

To: _____

You make my life AWESOME in more ways than I can count (and—not to brag—but I can count pretty high). But for starters, here's 5 of 'em:

1._____

2._____

3._____

4._____

5._____

I bow to your AWESOMENESS—now and forever.

From: _____

YOU'RE
MORE THAN
MAGNIFICENT.
YOU'RE
Magnifidollar.

To: a freakishly AWESOME
person named _____

Thank you for always _____

_____

_____

and for proving, once and for all, that _____

_____

_____

You're smashing. And that's final.

Love: _____

I LIKE
THE CUT
OF YOUR
JIB.

To: _____

I bet if you look up "AWESOME" in the dictionary,
there's a diagram of your DNA. Made by scientists.
Who know things.

As long as I live, I'll never forget the AWESOME way you

_____

_____and _____

_____

THANK YOU barely covers it.

XO. _____

EVEN YOUR
MEDIOCRE IDEAS
are
MENSA-LEVEL
HOTNESS.

80 92

To: _____

FACT:

The world is better with your AWESOMENESS in it.

Thank you for reminding me that _____

_____

and for sharing your _____

_____

Stay shiny and shimmery-bright.

From: _____

YOU'RE
THE GRAND PRIZE
AND THE
HONORABLE
MENTION.

1st

I hereby decree _____

to be Completely and Utterly AWESOME

in Every Conceivable Way.

This proclamation goes into worldwide effect on

_____ at _____ am / pm.

Those who disagree with my proclamation can,

legally speaking, get lost.

Yours
Sincerely,

_____

CEO and President of _____

I WANT
TO DANCE
TO THE BEAT
OF YOUR
BRILLIANCE.

To: _____

Life isn't always easy—but you're always AWESOME.

I admire the way you _____,

even when things are tough.

And if I were President of the World, you'd win a prize for

_____.

Keep on trucking, _____,

You've got a major fan, right here.

Love: _____

YOUR ACUMEN IS MAKING ME WEAK IN THE KNEES.

Dear: _____

If I could, I'd rent an airplane

and write **You're AWESOME!** in the clouds.

But, shucks! I forgot to renew my pilot's license.

Instead… here's a quick note:

_____

_____

_____

Your brilliance knows no bounds.

Love: _____

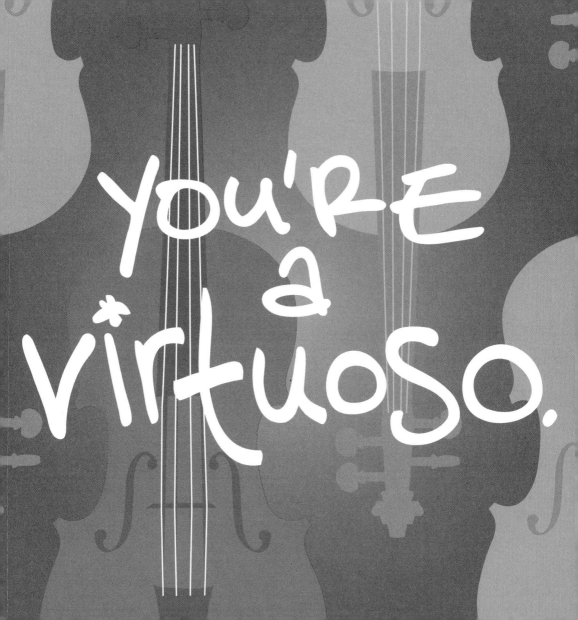

Dear: _____

I'm not sure how you got so AWESOME—

but I'm really glad you did.

I think it's fan-freakin'-tastic that you _____

_____

and I'm so proud of the way you _____

_____.

You are the most _____ person I know.

Put simply? You rule.

XO. _____

YOU'RE
ALL THAT
& A
BAG
OF

SWEET POTATO CHIPS

To: _____

You're AWESOME because_____

_____

_____ .

Ooh! And one more thing_____

_____

_____ .

From: _____

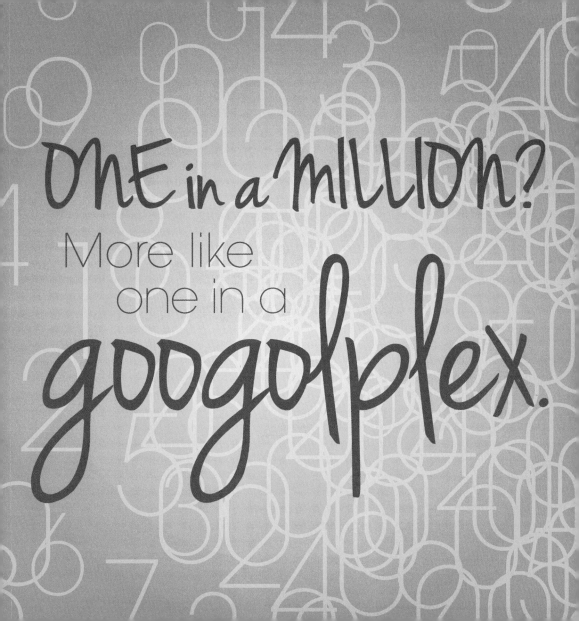

To: _____

In case you forgot: I think you're unbelievably AWESOME.

I appreciate the way you _____

_____.

And how you always _____

_____.

Thank you for adding so much _____

_____ to my life.

Love: _____

YOU'RE LUMINOUS—
JUST LOOK AT YOU GLOW!

To: _____

You make my life AWESOME in more ways than I can count (and—not to brag—but I can count pretty high). But for starters, here's 5 of 'em:

1._____

2._____

3._____

4._____

5._____

I bow to your AWESOMENESS—now and forever.

From: _____

YOU SHOULD CHARGE COLD HARD CASH TO LET PEOPLE BASK IN YOUR GLORY.

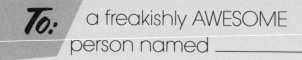

To: a freakishly AWESOME
person named _____

Thank you for always _____

_____

_____

and for proving, once and for all, that _____

_____

_____.

You're smashing. And that's final.

Love: _____

YOU BLOW MY MIND LIKE A CAT 5 HURRICANE.

To: _____

I bet if you look up "AWESOME" in the dictionary, there's a diagram of your DNA. Made by scientists. Who know things.

As long as I live, I'll never forget the AWESOME way you

_____

_____ and _____

_____

THANK YOU barely covers it.

XO. _____

YOU'RE LIKE
A LASER BEAM
IN THE NIGHT:
so freakin'
bright!

To: _____

FACT:

The world is better with your AWESOMENESS in it.

Thank you for reminding me that _____

_____

and for sharing your_____

_____

Stay shiny and shimmery-bright.

From: _____

I'M SO HAPPY WE'RE SHARING THE PLANET IN THE SAME

Historical Era

To: _____

Life isn't always easy—but you're always AWESOME.

I admire the way you _____,

even when things are tough.

And if I were President of the World, you'd win a prize for

_____.

Keep on trucking, _____.

You've got a major fan, right here.

Love: _____

You're
a miracle
machine.

If I could, I'd rent an airplane

and write **You're AWESOME!** in the clouds.

But, shucks! I forgot to renew my pilot's license.

Instead... here's a quick note:

_____

_____

_____

Your brilliance knows no bounds.

Love: _____

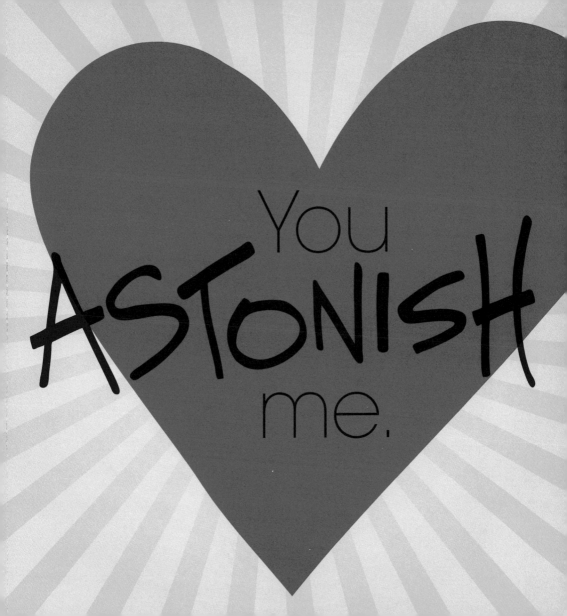

Dear: _____

I'm not sure how you got so AWESOME—

but I'm really glad you did.

I think it's fan-freakin'-tastic that you _____

_____

and I'm so proud of the way you _____

_____.

You are the most _____ person I know.

Put simply? You rule.

XO. _____

To: _____

You're AWESOME because _____

_____

_____ .

Ooh! And one more thing _____

_____

_____ .

From: _____

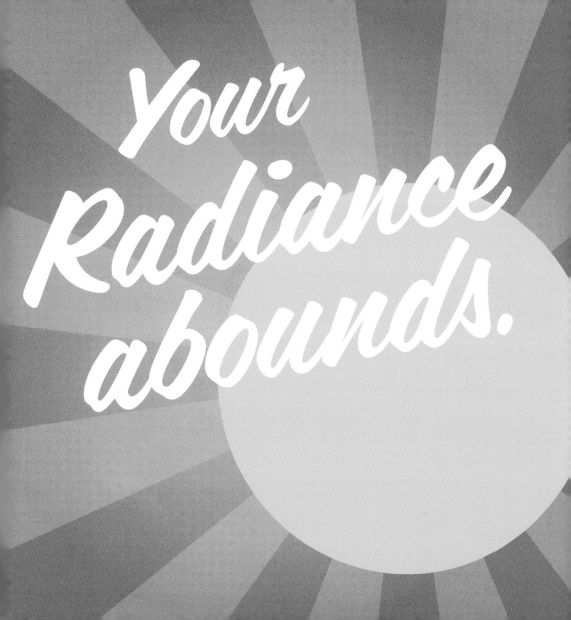

Your Radiance abounds.

To: _____

In case you forgot: I think you're unbelievably AWESOME.

I appreciate the way you _____

_____ .

And how you always _____

_____ .

Thank you for adding so much _____

_____ to my life.

Love: _____

YOU

ARE A CAUSE

for

celebration.

To: _____

You make my life AWESOME in more ways than I can
count (and—not to brag—but I can count pretty high).
But for starters, here's 5 of 'em:

1._____

2._____

3._____

4._____

5._____

I bow to your AWESOMENESS—now and forever.

From: _____

NO WONDER
THE PLANET'S
GETTING WARMER.
YOUR IDEAS
ARE SO FREAKIN'
Hot!

To: a freakishly AWESOME
person named _____

Thank you for always _____

_____

_____

and for proving, once and for all, that _____

_____

_____

You're smashing. And that's final.

Love: _____

I WANT TO ORBIT
AROUND YOUR

Splendor

LIKE A SATELLITE.

To: _____

I bet if you look up "AWESOME" in the dictionary, there's a diagram of your DNA. Made by scientists. Who know things.

As long as I live, I'll never forget the AWESOME way you

_____

_____ and _____

_____

THANK YOU barely covers it.

XO. _____

You ooze
INGENUITY.

2 cm

1 cm

8 cm

To: _____

FACT:

The world is better with your AWESOMENESS in it.

Thank you for reminding me that _____

_____

and for sharing your_____

_____ .

Stay shiny and shimmery-bright.

From: _____

WELCOME TO
Awesometown, USA.

♥

Population: YOU.

I hereby decree _____

to be Completely and Utterly AWESOME

in Every Conceivable Way.

This proclamation goes into worldwide effect on

_____ at _____ am / pm.

Those who disagree with my proclamation can,

legally speaking, get lost.

Yours
Sincerely,

_____

CEO and President of _____

To: _____

Life isn't always easy—but you're always AWESOME.

I admire the way you _____,

even when things are tough.

And if I were President of the World, you'd win a prize for

_____.

Keep on trucking, _____.

You've got a major fan, right here.

Love: _____

Dear: _____

If I could, I'd rent an airplane

and write **You're AWESOME!** in the clouds.

But, shucks! I forgot to renew my pilot's license.

Instead… here's a quick note:

_____

_____

_____

Your brilliance knows no bounds.

Love: _____

Dear: _____

I'm not sure how you got so AWESOME—

but I'm really glad you did.

I think it's fan-freakin'-tastic that you _____

_____

and I'm so proud of the way you _____

_____.

You are the most _____ person I know.

Put simply? You rule.

XO. _____

YOU JUST
REVIVED
MY FAITH in
HUMANITY.

To: _____

You're AWESOME because _____

_____

_____

Ooh! And one more thing _____

_____

_____

From: _____

To: _____

You make my life AWESOME in more ways than I can count (and—not to brag—but I can count pretty high). But for starters, here's 5 of 'em:

1. _____

2. _____

3. _____

4. _____

5. _____

I bow to your AWESOMENESS—now and forever.

From: _____

To: a freakishly AWESOME
person named _____

Thank you for always _____

_____

_____

and for proving, once and for all, that _____

_____

_____

You're smashing. And that's final.

Love: _____

WHEN DID
YOU GET SO
WONDERFULLY
wise?

To: _____

I bet if you look up "AWESOME" in the dictionary, there's a diagram of your DNA. Made by scientists. Who know things.

As long as I live, I'll never forget the AWESOME way you

_____

_____and_____

_____.

THANK YOU barely covers it.

XO. _____

YOU'RE
THE CAKE AND
THE ICING—
WITH A SPRINKLE OF
holy-
cowza.

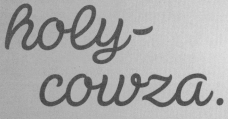

To: _____

FACT:

The world is better with your AWESOMENESS in it.

Thank you for reminding me that _____

_____

and for sharing your _____

_____.

Stay shiny and shimmery-bright.

From: _____

I hereby decree _____

to be Completely and Utterly AWESOME

in Every Conceivable Way.

This proclamation goes into worldwide effect on

_____at_____ am / pm.

Those who disagree with my proclamation can,

legally speaking, get lost.

Yours
Sincerely,

_____

CEO and President of_____

ARE YOU PUTTING *AWESOME DROPS* IN YOUR COFFEE AGAIN?

(I can tell.)

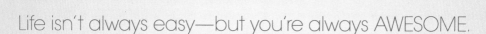 **To:** _____

Life isn't always easy—but you're always AWESOME.

I admire the way you _____,

even when things are tough.

And if I were President of the World, you'd win a prize for

_____.

Keep on trucking, _____.

You've got a major fan, right here.

 *Love:* _____

MAY I
HAVE ONE
OF YOU IN
EVERY
FLAVOR?

Dear: _____

If I could, I'd rent an airplane

and write **You're AWESOME!** in the clouds.

But, shucks! I forgot to renew my pilot's license.

Instead… here's a quick note:

_____

_____

_____

Your brilliance knows no bounds.

Love: _____

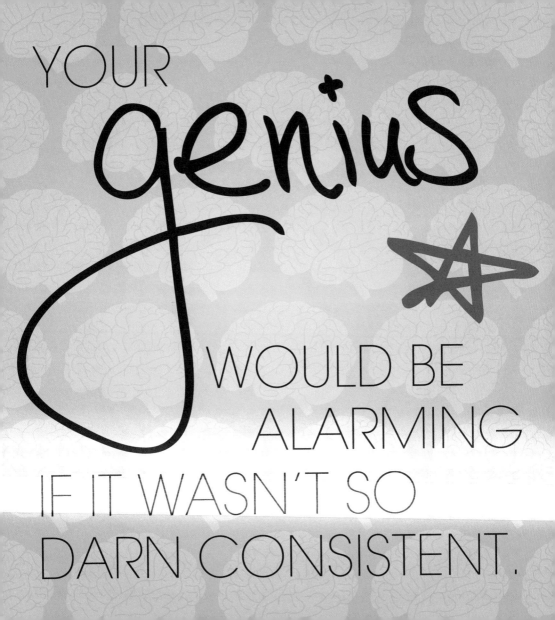

Dear: _____

I'm not sure how you got so AWESOME—

but I'm really glad you did.

I think it's fan-freakin'-tastic that you _____

_____

and I'm so proud of the way you _____

_____

You are the most _____ person I know.

Put simply? You rule.

XO. _____

To: _____

You're AWESOME because_____

_____

_____ .

Ooh! And one more thing_____

_____

_____ .

From: _____

GRATITUDE

So many people to thank.
Just one page to do it. Here goes!

REBECCA POLLOCK. My Visual Queen! Thank you for taking my words and creating such incredible illustrations. This book wouldn't exist without you.

KRISTINA HOLMES. I couldn't wish for a more diligent and devoted literary agent. I bow to thee.

SHANA AND DEIRDRE at Sourcebooks. Thank you for saying YES to Awesomery— and for making my dreams of becoming a published author come true.

DANIELLE LAPORTE, DYANA VALENTINE, ERIKA LYREMARK, SARAH VON BARGEN, MICHELLE WARD, AND HIRO BOGA. Thank you for inspiring me to make good art. Always.

MOM, DAD, BEN, AND OLIVIA. I'm so honored to share your DNA.

JEFF. Thank you for the copious encouragement. And for all the snuggles.

MY BLOG READERS, WORKSHOP STUDENTS, CLIENTS, AND INTERNET BUDDIES.
YOU... are all AWESOME.

ABOUT THE AUTHOR

ALEXANDRA FRANZEN is a writer, teacher, and creative minx based in Minneapolis (mostly). She's extremely proud of the fact that she quit her "real job" in public broadcasting to become a full-time wordsmith. She's also extremely proud of the fact that she can (almost) do the splits.

Alexandra has been spotlighted on over 50 blogs and podcasts on creativity and entrepreneurship, and in a handful of books, including *Grow Your Handmade Business*, *When Talent Isn't Enough*, and *The Declaration of You!*

She writes about life, love, work, and ecstatic self-expression at **AlexandraFranzen.com**.

Photograph by Jenn Kelly